The Student Loa.. ... .

Parent Borrowers and

Cosigners

Contents

Disclaimer

I'm an attorney, and I wouldn't be a true attorney if I didn't start this off with some important disclaimers:

This book is not an advertisement.

The material contained in this book is for informational purposes only and does not constitute legal advice. Reading this book is not a substitute for obtaining legal advice from an attorney.

Reading this book does not create an attorney-client relationship. This book is not intended to create, and does not constitute, a contract for representation by Adam S. Minsky, Esq.

The laws governing student loans are constantly changing, so I cannot guarantee that the material and information contained in this book is correct, complete, or up-to-date at the time that you read it.

There. Don't we all feel better now?

Introduction

I am a student loan lawyer. My entire practice is devoted entirely to assisting student loan borrowers.

When I say that, most people think of recent graduates – in their mid-to-late 20's, saddled with student loan debt, struggling to get a job in a sluggish economy, and trying to navigate a confusing student loan servicing and collections system. Those are some of my clients.

But the cost of education often falls on others besides the student going to school. These are parents, siblings, aunts, uncles, cousins, or friends of the student. They somehow got saddled with student debt for someone *else's* college education, and then they get in trouble.

What? How is that even possible? There are two main ways that people find themselves in student debt on behalf of someone else:

1. Taking out a federal **Parent PLUS loan**. This is a specific (and, in my opinion, rather nightmarish) type of federal student loan where the parent goes into debt on behalf of the student.

2. **Cosigning** a private student loan. A cosigner endorses the loan contract right along with the borrower. But many cosigners don't understand that they are, by law, equally responsible for the entire underlying debt.

These two education financing scenarios can cause significant unforeseen problems for the non-student borrower, and navigating your way out of trouble can be horrendous. There are very few resources out there to help student loan borrowers, and even fewer for struggling parents and cosigners.

That's why I wrote this book. I've divided it into two major parts. Part I is devoted entirely to Parent PLUS loans. Part II is about cosigners of private student loans.

PART I: Parent PLUS Loans

What are Parent PLUS Loans?

Parent PLUS loans are federal student loans where the *parent*, not the student, is the borrower. A lot of parents think that by taking out this type of loan, they are "cosigning" a loan for their child (the student), and the student will ultimately be responsible for repaying the loan. This is not true (and that's not even how cosigning works… more on that in Part II). While some Parent PLUS loans can have a second "endorser" that is similar to a cosigner, the vast majority of Parent PLUS loans are meant to be repaid by one person: the parent.

Here's the bottom line when it comes to Parent PLUS loans:

The parent who takes out the Parent PLUS loan is the "borrower," and the parent alone is legally responsible for repayment of the loan. The student is not the borrower, and has no legal responsibility whatsoever to repay the Parent PLUS loan.

That means that you, the parent, must repay the Parent PLUS loan. If you fall behind on the loan or go into default, the federal government will pursue you, not the student.

Parent PLUS loans come in two varieties: FFEL, or Direct.

Federal Family Education Loan (FFEL) Program

Until 2010, many Parent PLUS loans were issued via the FFEL program, where banks or other private lenders issued federally-guaranteed loans. The program was eliminated in 2010, so if you took out all of your Parent PLUS loans after that, you can skip to the Direct Federal Loans section. The FFEL program works like this:

1. A private entity lent you money. This was your FFEL lender.

2. If you default on the loan, it is guaranteed, or backed, by a state agency or non-profit organization, called a **guarantor** or **guaranty agency**. The guarantor pays the FFEL lender for the remaining balance of your loan, and you in turn owe the guarantor, rather than the original lender.
3. Guarantors are, in turn, insured by the federal government. If the guaranty agency fails to adequately resolve the default, the agency can assign the loan to the U.S. Department of Education for collection.

Even though FFEL lenders are private, these loans are considered federal because the federal government guarantees them. The loan program is governed by federal law. It's a convoluted system that is thankfully not used anymore, but there are still millions of borrowers who have FFEL loans, including many parent borrowers.

Direct Federal Loans

All Parent PLUS loans issued since 2010, and some Parent PLUS loans issued before then, are Direct federal loans. The money for these loans is provided directly by the U.S. Department of Education. There are no private lenders or guaranty agencies involved. However, day-to-day billing operations are handled by private loan servicing companies contracted by the Department of Education. There are many different loan servicers.

TIP: If you're not sure whether your Parent PLUS loans are FFEL or Direct loans, you can check the National Student Loan Data System (available at www.nslds.ed.gov). Direct loans will be listed as "Direct" in the database. FFEL loans will either be listed as "FFEL" or will just not have the word "Direct" in front of the loan name.

There's another type of "PLUS" loan called a Graduate PLUS loan. This loan falls under the same loan program (the PLUS program) but it is provided to graduate and professional students, such as law students or medical students. Graduate PLUS loans are **not** the same as Parent PLUS loans; Graduate PLUS loans are lent directly to the student. Remember the underlying rule about a Parent PLUS loan:

The parent who takes out the Parent PLUS loan is the borrower and is solely legally responsible for repayment of the loan. The student is not the borrower, and has no legal responsibility whatsoever to repay the Parent PLUS loan.

TIP: If you have a PLUS loan but you're not sure if it's a Graduate PLUS loan or a Parent PLUS loan, you can check the National Student Loan Data System (available at www.nslds.ed.gov). Graduate PLUS loans will have the word "Grad" or "Graduate" in the description of the loan type. Parent PLUS loans will just say "Direct PLUS" or "FFEL PLUS." You can also contact your loan servicer for additional information.

What Makes Parent PLUS Loans Different?

Parent PLUS loans are similar to other federal student loans in some key ways, both good and bad:

- Parent PLUS loans, like other federal student loans, are contractual, but the PLUS program is governed by federal laws and regulations. This is different from a purely private student loan, which is governed by a private contract.
- Like other federal student loans, Parent PLUS loans have relatively generous deferment and forbearance options (which allow a borrower to postpone making loan payments for a limited time) if you experience economic hardship. However, interest continues to accrue during periods of deferment and forbearance, and, as explained below, Parent PLUS loans have very high interest rates.
- Because they are federal loans, Parent PLUS loans are subject to the severe collection powers of the federal government if the loan goes into default. These include wage garnishment, tax refund interception, and, if the parent is disabled or retired, the offset of Social Security benefits. There is no statute of limitations on the collection of this type of debt, meaning it will follow the parent to the grave. And discharging Parent PLUS loans in bankruptcy, while not completely impossible, can be exceptionally difficult.

But that's where the similarities to other federal student loans end. Parent PLUS loans have some key characteristics that really set them apart:

- Parent PLUS loans have very high interest rates, the highest among any type of federal student loan. As of the fall of 2014, interest rates for Parent PLUS loans are 7.21%. However, it is common for older Parent PLUS loans to have interest rates in excess of 8%. Under current law, they may rise as high as 10.5% in the coming years. That's $1,050 in interest per year for every $10,000 disbursement. For $100,000 in Parent PLUS loans, that's $10,500 per year in interest.

- Parent PLUS loans incur origination fees, which can be over 4% of the original loan balance. Combined with the high interest rate, this makes PLUS loans exceptionally expensive.
- Parent PLUS loans are not eligible for income-driven repayment, such as Income-Based Repayment (IBR) or Pay-As-You-Earn (PAYE). This is particularly problematic for parents who take out large Parent PLUS loans and intend to retire in the relatively near future. That may no longer be possible with huge monthly loan bills. Parent PLUS loans *can* be repaid under Income-Contingent Repayment (ICR), an older and less-favorable income-driven option, under certain circumstances that involve Direct loan consolidation, but ICR can still be tough for many parents. (I'll talk more about ICR and Direct loan consolidation a bit later.)
- Unlike most federal student loans, the federal government now requires parents to pass a credit check in order to obtain a Parent PLUS loan.
- Parents can borrow up to the cost of attendance, as determined by the school, minus any other financial assistance the student has received. Most other federal student loan programs have lower caps. This means that Parents can obtain very large Parent PLUS loan disbursements each year, depending on the circumstances.
- Unlike federal student loans where the student is the borrower, repayment of the Parent PLUS loan begins **immediately** after the loan has been disbursed. For other student loans, payments are deferred while the student is in school at least half-time.

What are the Repayment Options for Parent PLUS Loans?

When it comes to repaying your Parent PLUS loans, you'll probably have several choices, but fewer than for other federal student loans, as Parent PLUS loans have several important restrictions.

TIP: The NSLDS database at www.nslds.ed.gov does not show your repayment plan. If you are currently in repayment and don't know what repayment plan you are on, you can contact your loan servicer, and they should be able to tell you.

Balance-Based Repayment

Most Parent PLUS loans will have to be repaid on a **balance-based** plan. These plans take into account the balance of the loan and the interest rate. Since we know that Parent PLUS loans tend to be disbursed in fairly large balances, and they have very high interest rates, the balance-based plans can be very expensive.

Let's say Sally takes out **$80,000** in Parent PLUS loans with an **8.5%** interest rate (fairly average for a Parent PLUS loan, depending on the loan program and year the loan was disbursed). We'll look at the various repayment plans to understand her options:

Balance-Based Level Repayment Plans are based on the loan balance and interest rate, with monthly payments spread out evenly over time. The repayment term can vary from 10 to 30 years, depending on your loan program. Longer repayment terms mean lower monthly payments, but cost more in total because it takes longer to pay the loan off.

For Sally, the 10-year Standard Level Repayment Plan would cost her roughly **$995** per month. Over 10 years, she would pay approximately **$119,000** in total.

A 25-year Extended Level Repayment Plan would cost Sally only **$650** per month, but over the course of the loan repayment term, she would pay a total of approximately **$193,000.** The price of lowering her monthly payments by about $350 per month is $74,000 in extra interest as compared to the 10-year repayment term.

Balance-Based Graduated Repayment Plans are also based on the loan balance and interest rate, but the monthly payments change over the repayment term. They are much lower early on, and gradually ramp up to compensate later. Many borrowers on these plans will pay more over the life of the loan than they would under the Level Repayment Plan options. Graduated Repayment Plan terms can be 10 or 25 years.

On a 10-year Graduated Repayment Plan, Sally's monthly payment would start at approximately **$585**, but would gradually increase to nearly **$1,750** towards the end of the repayment term. After 10 years, she would have paid approximately **$130,000.** That's over 150% of the original loan balance.

For a 25-Year Extended Graduated Plan, her payment would start at approximately **$570**, but would increase to nearly **$850**. Over 25 years, she will pay approximately **$207,000.** That's $77,000 more than the already expensive 10-year Graduated Repayment Plan, and $14,000 more than the 25-year Level Repayment Plan.

Graduated repayment options are designed to ease the burden at the beginning of the loan repayment period, but the price for early relief is higher payments down the line, and a larger amount paid in total over the course of the repayment term.

Graduated plans are, in my opinion, terrible options for Parent PLUS borrowers, especially the 25-year option. When parents take out PLUS loans, they are typically near the height of their careers, usually between the ages of 40 and 60. By structuring their repayment plans to be much more expensive in five, 10, or 20 years, parents are setting themselves up for disaster if they experience a drop in income or ever expect to retire.

Income-Driven Repayment

Income-Driven Repayment Plans account for income, family size, and federal poverty levels. For many student borrowers, these are the only affordable repayment plans. **However, Parent PLUS loans are generally not eligible for income-driven repayment**. This is one of the most significant pitfalls of the Parent PLUS loan.

That said, there is an option. Parent PLUS loans can be **consolidated** via the federal Direct Loan Consolidation program. Direct Consolidation loans that repaid Parent PLUS loans after July 1, 2006 can be placed on the **Income-Contingent Repayment (ICR) plan**. This is the least-generous of the income-driven repayment programs, but it can be more affordable than a balance-based repayment plan for some Parent PLUS borrowers.

> *TIP: Parent PLUS loans are never eligible for the Income-Based Repayment (IBR) plan or the Pay-As-You-Earn (PAYE) plan, even if you consolidate them. IBR and PAYE are cheaper than ICR, but Parent PLUS loans are locked out of these plans.*

Here's how ICR works:

On ICR, your federal loan servicer will consider your total federal student loan debt, your annual gross taxable income, and your family size. Monthly payments on ICR are capped at 20% of the borrower's *discretionary income*, which is the amount of adjusted gross income (as shown on the borrower's tax return) above the poverty limit, adjusted for family size. The repayment period is up to 25 years. Any balance that remains after the repayment period is forgiven, though the forgiven amount may be treated as taxable income.

If Sally consolidated her $80,000 in PLUS loans at an 8.5% interest rate through the Direct Consolidation program after July 1, 2006, and she enrolled in in the ICR plan, her payment will be driven by her adjusted gross income and family size. **Under ICR, Sally's loan servicer will consider her spouse's income along with her own, but only if they files taxes jointly.**

Let's do a few estimates, to show how Sally's loan payments may change depending on her income levels. We'll assume that when Sally enters repayment on her Parent PLUS loan (an $80,000 balance with an interest rate of 8.5%) she and her spouse are at the height of their careers. With an annual taxable household income of $100,000 and a household size of two, her monthly ICR payment will be approximately **$1,110.** That's more expensive than her payments under the 10-year or 25-year level repayment plans, so there's no reason for Sally to select ICR right now.

If Sally selects ICR, her payments will adjust each year as her income changes, and she'll need to provide annual documentation of her income to determine her monthly payments for the next 12 months. If Sally and her spouse cut back their hours at work, and their annual household taxable income decreases to $60,000, her monthly payment will be approximately **$740.** This is cheaper than her monthly payment under the 10-year level plan, but more expensive than the 25-year level plan.

Let's say Sally and her spouse experience yet another significant drop in income. Maybe she lost her job, or perhaps she retired and now receives only retirement benefits. Now her household income is $30,000 (she still has a household size of two). Under these circumstances, Sally's monthly payment under ICR would be only approximately **$240** per month. This is far cheaper than any other repayment plan option available to her.

So what's the takeaway from this? ICR is not perfect, especially for parents with a large consolidated Parent PLUS loan balance *and* high annual household income. However, ICR can be a lifesaver for Parent PLUS borrowers who experience a significant drop in income.

But remember, if you have Parent PLUS loans, you have to consolidate these loans through the Direct Consolidation program in order to be eligible for ICR. How do you do that?

Consolidation

In order to even get onto the ICR plan with Parent PLUS loans, you must consolidate these loans through the federal Direct Consolidation program. And you must have done this *after* July 1, 2006.

When you take out a federal Direct Consolidation loan, the U.S. Department of Education pays off your individual federal loans and issues a new federal student loan with their combined balance. Consolidation has a few inherent benefits: it can simplify repayment if you have multiple federal loans with multiple servicing companies; you'll end up with one loan, one payment, and one federal loan servicer. Consolidation also provides a uniform fixed interest rate based on the weighted average of all the original loans.

But, if you have already spent a significant amount of time in repayment on your existing federal loans, consolidation restarts the clock on your repayment term, since consolidation technically results in a new loan. If you've been in repayment on any of your loans for a while, this could be a drawback. For example, if you are 10 years into a 25-year Extended Level Repayment Plan when you consolidate your loans, you might place your new consolidation loan onto a new 25-year repayment plan. As a result, you would be in repayment for 35 years in total.

Here's how consolidation works. To get a Direct Consolidation loan, you can submit a federal Direct Consolidation loan application either online, or on paper. Applications usually take 4-8 weeks to process. Once approved, there is no grace period for the new consolidated loan before repayment begins. Like the Parent PLUS loans themselves, the consolidation loan enters repayment as soon it is issued, and payments are usually due the following month. You will have to select a repayment plan for your loan from the available options (you can submit your repayment plan application right along with your consolidation application).

The U.S. Department of Education now allows borrowers applying for new Direct Consolidation loans to choose their Direct Consolidation loan servicer. This is a huge change. I hope it will really benefit borrowers, since borrowers used to have no say at all in selecting their servicer. Unfortunately, it only applies to new Direct Consolidation loans. Borrowers who are consolidating can select from one of the following four servicers:

FedLoan Servicing is the Direct Loan servicing branch of the Pennsylvania Higher Education Assistance Association (PHEAA), a state agency. They have a special department for people who are on track for Public Service Loan Forgiveness (which we'll cover later).

Great Lakes Higher Education is a nonprofit organization based in Madison, Wisconsin. In addition to their servicing operations for the Direct Loan program, they serve as a guaranty agency (with an internal collections department) for the FFEL federal loan program.

Nelnet is a for-profit company based in Nebraska. They have dozens of subsidiaries and they service student loans throughout the United States and Canada.

Navient is a for-profit company based in Pennsylvania. It recently split from Sallie Mae and became a separate company. Sallie Mae is now simply a private loan lender (it no longer services Direct federal loans).

Under current law, you cannot consolidate your private student loans along with your federal student loans. Only federal student loans can be consolidated into the federal Direct Consolidation loan program.

TIP: Be careful about including non-Parent PLUS loans in your consolidation loan. As mentioned above, Parent PLUS loans are never eligible for the Income-Based Repayment (IBR) plan or the Pay-As-You-Earn (PAYE) plan, which are cheaper plans than Income-Contingent Repayment (ICR). If you have other federal student loans besides your Parent PLUS loans, those loans may be eligible for IBR or PAYE. If you consolidate Parent PLUS loans with these other loans, it can make the entire consolidation ineligible for IBR and PAYE. If you keep the two loan groups separate, however, you could put your consolidated Parent PLUS loans on the ICR plan, and repay the other federal student loans under the IBR or PAYE plan (if eligible).

TIP: To learn more about federal Direct loan consolidation, visit www.studentloans.gov.

Can Parent PLUS Loans be Reassigned, Discharged, or Forgiven?

Reassignment

This is one of the most common questions I get in my practice from borrowers: can't the student just take over the Parent PLUS loan, or consolidate it with the student's existing student loans? The answer, unfortunately, is a resounding **no**. Parent PLUS loan can never be reassigned or taken over by the student/child. Of course, there's nothing preventing the student (or anyone else, for that matter) from repaying the Parent PLUS loan on behalf of the parent. But until the loan is completely paid off, all **legal responsibility** for the loan remains with the parent borrower.

Discharge

In general, Parent PLUS Loans cannot be discharged, absent exceptional circumstances. For instance, if the parent borrower becomes totally and permanently disabled, he or she can apply for a disability discharge of their PLUS loan. If the child for whom the PLUS loan was disbursed dies, the parent can apply for a death discharge. However, the parent cannot apply for a disability discharge if the child becomes disabled. There are also limited administrative discharge options for loans that were taken our fraudulently. Very occasionally, borrowers can discharge student loans (including Parent PLUS loans) in bankruptcy, but it is very difficult for student and parent borrowers to qualify for a bankruptcy discharge.

> *TIP: If you're thinking about discharging your Parent PLUS loan, now is a good time to speak with an attorney who specializes in student loans or bankruptcy.*

Public Service Loan Forgiveness (PSLF)

This is probably the most well-known loan forgiveness program currently available. PSLF is only available to borrowers working full-time in qualifying public service employment. Fortunately, this does include certain Parent PLUS borrowers. Under PSLF, the borrower makes qualifying payments for 10 years, and the outstanding loan balance is forgiven. The forgiven balance is not taxed, which is a significant benefit compared to other types of loan forgiveness.

The eligibility requirements for PSLF are a little tricky. Only Direct federal loans are eligible, and you need to make repayments using one of the income-driven options or the 10-year Standard plan. For Parent PLUS borrowers, this means you must consolidate your Parent PLUS loans through the Direct Consolidation program after July 1, 2006 and select the Income-Contingent Repayment (ICR) plan. You must work full-time in public service (a government job or a position at certain domestic nonprofit organizations). And you must meet all of these requirements for 120 monthly payments over the course of 10 years. Since the program has only been around since 2007, we won't know how PSLF actually works out until the first eligible borrowers apply for forgiveness in 2017. But a lot of borrowers stand to benefit, including some parent borrowers, as long as they do everything right.

> *TIP: For more information on Public Service Loan Forgiveness, you can check out FedLoan Servicing at www.MyFedLoan.org, which has some good information on program eligibility.*

Repayment Plan-Based Loan Forgiveness

The Income-Contingent Repayment (ICR) plan has built-in loan forgiveness after 25 years of repayment. In addition to employment-based forgiveness, by consolidating their Parent PLUS loans through the Direct Consolidation program, Parent PLUS borrowers can place their consolidation loan on the ICR plan. Remember that ICR is only available for loans consolidated after July 1, 2006. Under ICR, any remaining balance is forgiven after 25 years of payments.

TIP: When a parent discharges his or her Parent PLUS loans, whether through bankruptcy, loan forgiveness, disability discharge, or some other means, there should be no direct consequences to the student.

What Happens if you Default on a Parent PLUS Loan?

If you start falling behind on your Parent PLUS loan payments, I'll be honest, it's not going to be pretty.

First, you enter a loan status called *delinquency*. You may accrue late fees, and the late payments may be reported to the credit bureaus, which can hurt your credit score. But the good news is that delinquency is generally fixable.

I've already written about repayment plan options for Parent PLUS loans, and you may find that Direct loan consolidation-plus-ICR can provide some relief. If that doesn't work, you can consider *deferment* or *forbearance* to postpone your payments. Just be careful…

Deferment and Forbearance

Deferments and forbearances allow borrowers to postpone their payments for specific reasons, including financial hardship or returning to school. While these options can provide crucial short-term relief for borrowers, they are poor long-term strategies for managing your loans. Deferment and forbearance options are generously available for federal student loans, but are typically more restrictive for private student loans.

For federal student loans, the main difference between deferment and forbearance is the handling of interest. For Parent PLUS loans, there is very little difference between a deferment and a forbearance in terms of the interest consequences because Parent PLUS loans are unsubsidized loans, meaning the government will never cover or waive interest accrual.

There are serious consequences of going into long-term deferment and forbearance. It's easy to forget about your loan when you don't have to make any payments. But while you're not paying much attention, interest is accruing, and your balance is increasing. Because of the high interest rates of Parent PLUS loans, the interest consequences can be hugely significant.

Let's compare two situations. Dan is a **student** borrower with a $60,000.00 federal student loan at a 4.5% interest rate. Dan goes into forbearance:

- After 6 months, he owes $61,350.
- After 12 months, he owes $62,700.00
- After 24 months, he owes $65,520.00
- After 36 months, he owes $68,470.00.

Dan's balance grew by over $8,000 (about 14% of the starting balance) over three years of forbearance. But Dan is a student borrower, so his interest rate is much lower than most Parent PLUS borrowers.

Now let's look at Sally, a **parent** borrower with a $60,000.00 Parent PLUS balance at the much higher interest rate of 8.5%. She has the same starting balance as Dan. Sally goes into forbearance:

- After 6 months, she owes $62,550.00
- After 12 months, she owes $65,100.00
- After 24 months, she owes $70,630.00
- After 36 months, she owes $76,640.00

So you can see, forbearance for Parent PLUS borrowers is much, much more expensive than for student borrowers, simply because of the interest rate. After three years of forbearance, Sally wound up with an additional $16,640.00 in accumulated interest on her loan, which is twice as much as Dan. That's nearly 28% higher than what she started with. If Dan's three-year forbearance was expensive, Sally's is just absurd.

Most federal loan deferments and forbearances max out at 36 months (to be clear, that's 36 months of deferment, plus 36 months of forbearance). So in the above example, Dan and Sally each bought three years of postponed payments, but at a very high price. Furthermore, all of the interest that accumulated during forbearance will be added to the principal balance, and interest will continue to accrue on that higher total principal balance. The overall loan balance will now grow at an even faster rate than before, and it will require larger monthly payments to keep up.

For most people, deferments and forbearances only make sense as a short-term measure. If you lose your job and need a few months to get back on your feet, or you have an unexpected expense that stretches you too thin for a month or two, they can be viable options to avoid falling behind on your payments and getting hit with late fees and negative credit reporting. But as soon as it's possible, get onto a workable repayment plan. If you don't, you'll be shocked at how much it will cost in the long run.

Federal Loan Default

If you can't fix the delinquency, you can't afford repayment, and you exhaust your deferment and forbearance options, you will eventually *default* on your loans. This means you've broken the loan contract. Typically, the entire balance of your loan becomes due immediately, in one lump sum. This is called *acceleration*. Default on federal loans (including Parent PLUS loans) typically occurs after 270 days of delinquency.

The consequences of federal loan default are serious. Here's a rundown:

- The entire balance of the loan becomes due at once. That includes the principal, the accumulated interest, and the penalties and late fees.

- The default will be reported to all major credit bureaus, which will impact your credit score in a big way.
- Without a court order, the federal government can seize your tax refund (if one is due to you) and apply it to your federal loan balance. They don't need to ask your permission; they just won't pay you the refund in the first place.
- Without a court order, the federal government can garnish your wages. (In contrast, a private lender must obtain a court judgment in order to do this.)
- Without a court order, the federal government can seize a certain portion of federal benefits, such as Social Security or other federal money owed to you.
- Federal law authorizes private collections agencies contracted with the federal government to tack on exorbitant collections costs (16.5% to 24.5% of the defaulted loan balance). This is how collections agencies profit off of defaulted borrowers. Even if you can resolve your default, you may be legally responsible for some or all of these additional costs.
- You cannot obtain new federal financial aid while you are in default. If you defaulted on your Parent PLUS loans while your child was in school, you won't be able to take out any new Parent PLUS loans while the loan remains in default. In fact, even if you resolve your default, you will be prohibited from taking out new Parent PLUS loans for a long time, because recent changes to federal law require a credit check for Parent PLUS borrowers.
- There is no statute of limitations on the collection of federal student loans, which means the federal government can pursue you for the rest of your life. That means that if your wages are being garnished and you cannot resolve the default, the garnishment may continue until you stop working, and then the federal government can offset a portion of your social security benefits during retirement. It just doesn't end.
- The federal government or federal loan guaranty agency can sue you in court. With a judgment from a court of law, the federal lender has even more powers to pursue you, such as by putting a lien on any property you own or seizing assets.

This is, of course, terrifying. But there is good news. You may be able to resolve your defaulted Parent PLUS loans and return them to good standing:

Resolving Federal Loan Default through Rehabilitation

A defaulted federal loan borrower can *rehabilitate* their federal student loan, bringing it out of default via a temporary monthly payment plan. By making 9 timely payments over the course of 10 months, followed by a transition period where the loan is placed with a new lender or servicer, a borrower can restore the loan to good standing.

Rehabilitation plans must be negotiated directly with the loan holders or their contracted debt collection agencies. The monthly payment amount for rehabilitation is negotiable to some extent. Loan holders may request a monthly rehabilitation payment based on the loan's balance, but borrowers have a right to a "reasonable and affordable" rehabilitation payment based on their financial circumstances.

Under recent changes to federal law, there are two main options for defining a "reasonable and affordable" rehabilitation payment:

- The collections agency can utilize a formula, similar to the income-driven repayment plan options, to calculate a monthly payment based on your income and family size.
- Alternatively, the collections agency can do a financial review of your household income and expenses. The review must be quite thorough and will likely require significant supporting documentation.

TIP: Which rehabilitation calculation option is best for you? It really depends on your circumstances at the time that you are seeking to rehabilitate your defaulted loan. Now might be a good time to talk to an attorney.

Rehabilitation has a unique advantage: the default notation is completely deleted from your credit report if you rehabilitate successfully. Other negative information, including the prior delinquencies, may remain in your credit history for some time, but rehabilitation can help to mitigate the worst of the credit impact.

TIP: Once you have rehabilitated a defaulted federal student loan, it cannot be rehabilitated again. It's a one-shot deal!

Resolving Federal Loan Default through Consolidation

Consolidation isn't just for borrowers in good standing. It can also help you get out of default. A Direct Consolidation loan essentially pays off your defaulted federal loans, just like it would if you were not in default. You would get a single, brand new federal student loan with one monthly payment, and the new consolidation loan would be in good standing.

Unlike rehabilitation, you do not need to make a series of payments before being allowed to consolidate. However, you must select an income-driven repayment plan (ICR, IBR, or PAYE) to pay off the consolidation loan. I may sound like a broken record here, but the same rule still applies to Parent PLUS borrowers: you will not be eligible for IBR or PAYE, so your only option is ICR.

The process is much faster than rehabilitation, but doesn't have the credit report default-deletion advantage.

REMEMBER: Be careful about including non-Parent PLUS loans in your consolidation loan. Parent PLUS loans are never eligible for the Income-Based Repayment (IBR) plan or the Pay-As-You-Earn (PAYE) plan, which are cheaper plans than Income-Contingent Repayment (ICR). If you consolidate your Parent PLUS loans with non-Parent-PLUS federal student loans, it could make the entire consolidation ineligible for IBR and PAYE, meaning ICR would be your only option. If you keep the two loan groups separate (either by doing two separate consolidations, or by only consolidating your Parent PLUS loans), you could put your consolidated Parent PLUS loans on the ICR plan, and repay the other federal student loans under the IBR or PAYE plan (if eligible).

Resolving Federal Loan Default through Settlement

It is difficult, but not impossible, to **settle** a defaulted federal student loan for less than the full balance due. These arrangements are governed by strict federal guidelines. The guidelines that apply to you, and the resulting settlement amount that you would have to pay, can vary depending on a variety of factors including your loan program, your loan holder, and your specific circumstances.

If you're considering a settlement, be prepared to pay a very sizeable portion of the loan balance in a lump-sum payment, and be prepared to pay it very quickly. Usually you'll have a window of 90 days or less, depending on the loan holder, and sometimes it's as short as 10 days. There are tax and credit report consequences to settlement as well, so you will want to consult with an attorney and a qualified tax expert before agreeing to anything.

TIP: Federal loan rehabilitation, consolidation, and settlement are complicated programs, and many factors can affect your eligibility. Some options may be better for you than others depending on your situation. If you are in default and are interested in a resolution, find a student loan attorney to help you navigate these options and advise you properly.

PART II: Cosigners

The Difference between Federal Student Loans and Private Student Loans

The first distinction between Parent PLUS loans and cosigned loans is that a Parent PLUS loan is a federal loan, whereas the vast majority of cosigned student loans are private (non-federal) loans. This means your cosigned loans are not disbursed or backed by the federal government. The distinction is hugely important because it will impact your rights and options.

Federal loans are either lent directly, or backed (guaranteed) by the federal government. Federal lenders provide many options to borrowers that allow for repayment flexibility and loan management. Interest rates also tend to be lower than private loans. Parent PLUS loans are, just to be absolutely clear, federal loans.

TIP: Don't know whether your student loans are federal or private? The National Student Loan Data System, available at www.nslds.ed.gov, is a database that lists all of your federal student loans. If you have a student loan that is not listed on the database, it is probably private.

Private loans are any type of educational debt that is *not* originated directly or "backed" by the federal government. Private loans are usually originated by banks or other commercial lenders (common private student loan lenders include Sallie Mae, Citibank, Discover, and Wells Fargo). Certain states also have state-based student lending programs. Sometimes, schools themselves have private financing programs where they lend money directly to their students.

While the terms and conditions of state-based student loans and institution-based student loans may differ from a purely commercial or bank-based student loan, they all essentially function as private student loans, simply because they are not originated or backed by the federal government.

While federal student loans offer a menu of repayment options and programs for managing federal student loan debt, private student loans are a whole different ballgame.

There are some benefits to private student loans:

- They are generally easier to obtain than federal student loans.
- You may not have to worry about college financial aid application cycles, or filling out the Free Application for Federal Student Aid (aka, the "FAFSA" form).
- Private student loans may offer greater flexibility for borrowers to shop around for a lower interest rate, whereas federal law determines federal student loan interest rates.
- If you default on your private student loans, the consequences may not be as immediate or as severe as a federal student loan default, at least in the beginning (more on that later, though).

But private student loans also have some serious drawbacks:

- They don't have the same built-in rights and protections as federal student loans.
- There are usually fewer, and less favorable, repayment plan options.
- Consolidation options are severely limited, so you may be stuck paying multiple private loan lenders and servicers.
- Depending on the loan terms, the lender may have broad discretion to decide whether you can postpone your payments during a financial hardship.
- Private lenders have been increasingly opting to default delinquent student loans and send them to collections agencies, rather than grant extended deferments, offer loan repayment modifications, or otherwise work with distressed

borrowers. We are starting to see some positive changes in this regard, but options for distressed private student loan borrowers remain quite limited.

Private student loans can be risky options to finance education in general, at least in my opinion.

Add in a cosigner, and things get even more complicated.

What it Means to be a "Cosigner"

Many private lenders require, or strongly encourage, the student borrower to obtain a ***cosigner***: someone who signs the loan contract right along with the student borrower. This happens for a few reasons:

- A student borrower may not have a good credit history, or any credit history at all.
- The private lender may offer a substantially lower interest rate for a cosigned loan, as compared to a loan that is just signed by the student alone.
- The private lender may just require a cosigner, period, as a matter of policy.

Statistics on private student loans are difficult to come by. But as a student loan attorney, the majority of private loan cases that come through my office have a cosigner. Private student loans that have a single signature (the student borrower) are rare.

There's a basic rule for cosigners that many people just do not fully understand or appreciate:

The cosigner is _fully_ legally responsible for the entire student loan, just as the borrower is.

I'll say it a different way: **you are not just being nice when you cosign. You are taking on the legal responsibility to pay the loan. It's exactly like you borrowed the money yourself.** This basic rule underlies all of your rights and responsibilities as a cosigner.

I feel bad for cosigners. The cosigner is usually a well-meaning parent, spouse, boyfriend, girlfriend, cousin, or friend. The cosigner is helping the student go to school to get an education. All the cosigner is doing, says the conventional wisdom, is enabling the student to get that loan that will pay for tuition, so that they can get that degree, get that good job, and get ahead in life. And the student will, of course, get employed upon graduation and promises (promises!) to pay the loan back. The cosigner won't even have to think about it.

Except, it doesn't always work that way. Let's go back to the basic cosigner rule: **The cosigner is fully legally responsible for the entire student loan, just as the borrower is.**

That means that if the student borrower doesn't pay the bill, the cosigner has to. If the student doesn't get that wonderful high-paying dream job after graduating, and she can't afford her repayment, the lender will come after both of you. If the borrower defaults on the loan, you default on the loan, too, and you'll get to experience the joys of debt collection right along with the borrower. Since these loans are private, neither of you gets the benefits of federal loans such as generous deferment and forbearance options, flexible repayment options, consolidation, and income-driven repayment. Moreover, some private loan contracts have provisions that will allow for adverse action against either (or both) of you if the other one does something that the lender doesn't like, such as miss a payment, file for bankruptcy, or die (I'm not joking—more on that, later).

Everyone enters into a cosigning relationship with the best of intentions. But I have seen cosigned student loans destroy relationships, end marriages, and sever family ties more times than I care to count, simply because no one fully understood the consequences of cosigning when they took out the loan in the first place. As with any situation, understand what you are doing before you agree to put your signature on a legal document. It may come back to bite you later, in a big, big way.

The Consequences of Delinquency and Default

Cosigning isn't usually much of a problem as long as the borrower is making timely payments on the cosigned student loan. Keep in mind, though, that most student loans have repayment terms of at least 10 years, and often much longer. That's plenty of time for something to go wrong.

Delinquency

Cosigning usually becomes an obvious issue when the borrower starts to fall behind on payments. Unlike federal loans, where the borrower can be behind on payments (delinquent) for up to 270 days before the loan defaults, private loans typically have a much shorter window of delinquency before entering default. The loan contract may specify how quickly a delinquent private student loan can go into default, but sometimes, just one missed payment is be enough to trigger it. Almost all private student loans will enter default much sooner than the 270 days window allowed for federal student loans. So to avoid default, you and the borrower will need to act quickly.

Just like with federal loans, a delinquency can be resolved prior to default. If the borrower is having trouble, remember that you, the cosigner, are on the hook as well, and you will suffer the same consequences as the borrower, including late fees, negative credit reporting, and potentially aggressive collections actions. Contact the private student loan servicer and consider your options:

- Make the past-due payments.
- Explore options to temporarily postpone the monthly payments or wipe out the past-due balance through a retroactive deferment or forbearance.

- See if the lender or servicer will agree to a loan modification, possibly by reducing the interest rate and corresponding monthly payment, or by getting on a reduced-payment plan, even if it's only temporary.

Ultimately, if the delinquency is not resolved, the private loan will go into default... for both of you.

Default

Just to review some terms: when a student loan enters **default**, it means that the loan contract has been broken. The entire balance of the loan becomes due immediately, in one lump sum (this is called **acceleration**). Regardless of who is to blame for the default, it affects both the borrower and the cosigner. It is not possible for the loan to remain in good standing for one signer, and not the other.

> *TIP: Many private lenders will refer to a private student loan default as a "charge-off," and that's how a default might even be reported to credit bureaus. For our purposes here, "default" and "charge-off" essentially mean the same thing: the loan is in bad standing, the contract is broken, and the entire balance is due.*

There are two key differences between private student loan defaults and federal student loan defaults.

- Private lenders do not have the same powers to pursue defaulted borrowers and cosigners as the federal government does. For example, a private lender cannot simply garnish your wages or seize your federal tax refund because it wants to. In order to force you to pay, the lender must first sue you in court and obtain a judgment against you. The lender must then use the power of the court to go after your wages and assets. This means that in the early stages of default, there's not a whole lot that the private lender can do to you. On the other hand, it makes private student loan lenders more likely to sue. And lenders frequently sue cosigners right along with the borrowers, because cosigners typically have more assets and more streams of income that they can pursue, compared to the borrower.

- Private student loans do not have the same avenues to resolve the default as federal student loans, such as rehabilitation or consolidation. You cannot consolidate private student loans through the federal Direct consolidation program. There are some private lenders that consolidate student loans, but these programs are rare, and they typically do not allow defaulted loans to be included in a consolidation. Private lenders that offer some sort of rehabilitation program are also extraordinarily rare (I have seen it, but in truly exceptional circumstances).

So what does this mean? Once a private student loan is in default, it usually cannot be restored to good standing. Generally, a defaulted private student loan borrower and cosigner will have only four broad options:

1. Pay in Full

This is the surest way to resolve the debt, but it is likely not an option for many people, including the cosigner.

2. Settle

Settlements resolve the debt without requiring the borrower or cosigner to pay the full balance. You pay a portion of the total debt, and the lender waives the remaining balance. The settlement amount must be negotiated, and the lender will require a payment made via a lump sum or a few limited installments. The exact amount of a settlement will vary depending on the type of loan, the loan holder's settlement criteria, and your own specific circumstances. As with federal student loans, there may be tax and credit report consequences to consider, so you will want to work with an attorney and consult with a tax expert to fully understand your rights and responsibilities.

3. Ignore, Wait, and Defend if Sued

Unlike federal student loans, private lenders are unable to "force" collections through tactics like administrative wage garnishment or by intercepting income streams without first suing the borrower and obtaining a judgment in court. There also is a statute of limitations that might apply to private student loans, which means that private lenders have a finite time period within which they must start trying to collect from you. If they try to collect from you outside of this time period, you may be able to raise the statute of limitations as a defense to a collections lawsuit. There are also other defenses to private student loan lawsuits. For example, some private student loans are bought and sold in the marketplace. If the current loan holder is different from the original lender, the current loan holder must prove in court that they are the valid holders of the original loan contract. Sometimes, they have difficulty doing that.

Since a private lender cannot force collections without first filing a lawsuit, winning, and obtaining a judgment, you could wait it out and hope for the best. This would be a roll of the dice. In a best-case scenario, you pay nothing and they do nothing, or they sue you and you win. In a worst-case scenario, you lose a lawsuit, get hit with a judgment, and the lender has significant powers to collect from you that they did not have before.

Ultimately, a lawsuit is very possible, and the lender will almost always sue the cosigner as well as the borrower. After all, the cosigner usually has more assets that the lender can pursue, such as higher wages or property. If you lose the lawsuit, the private lender could then use power of the courts to garnish your wages, place liens on your property, or seize certain assets, depending on the laws of your state. Thus there could be significant risk to ignoring the debt.

4. Make payments, either to yourself or to the loan holder

Rather than completely ignoring the debt, you and the borrower can save up for a potential settlement by making "payments" to yourselves and growing a settlement fund in a safe, interest-bearing account. Then if you are pursued in court, you have some cash to work with.

Alternatively, it might be possible to negotiate a repayment arrangement with the loan holder, either temporarily or on a long-term basis. An installment arrangement would not resolve the default, and it would not guarantee that the lender will not sue you. In some states, it could restart the clock on the statute of limitations. So this option carries some significant risk, as well. But it could also provide an incentive for the lender not to sue you, since it's cheaper for them to obtain voluntary payments than to pay a law firm to file a lawsuit.

TIP: Your legal rights and options will depend on your specific circumstances, the language in your loan contract, and the law that governs your situation. The ideal option for you may not be ideal for someone else. If you have a defaulted student loan, federal or private, you should consult with a qualified attorney to help you navigate the situation.

The "Death and Bankruptcy Clause"

Want to know my absolute least favorite thing about cosigned private student loans?

Many private student loan contracts have a tiny little clause, hidden away in the obscure depths of the fine print. It's written in more formal language, but it basically says that *if the cosigner or the borrower dies or declares bankruptcy, the entire balance of the loan is due immediately.* Technically, it's not a default, but if you can't pay the entire loan balance right then, it will go into default and collections.

Say you're the borrower, the loan is in good standing, and you're making your payments every month. You have good credit, a decent-paying job, and everything is swell. Your cosigner (a friend, a family member, or an ex-boyfriend or ex-girlfriend) declares bankruptcy and cannot get this loan discharged in the bankruptcy process, which is fairly typical. You will get a call from your lender, or maybe even a collections agency, telling you to pay up because the entire loan balance is due. You did nothing wrong. In fact, you did everything right. Your cosigner just triggered the death and bankruptcy clause, and now you're out of luck.

Or even more horrifying, say your cosigner dies. While you are dealing with the emotional upheaval of losing a close friend or family member, you get a call from your lender or a collections agency: pay up, the entire loan balance is due. No, you did nothing wrong, and yes, this is horrible timing. But your cosigner just triggered the death and bankruptcy clause, and now your loan is due in full.

The most upsetting scenario for me is the one where the borrower is a soldier, goes off to fight in a war, and gets killed in action. The cosigner is the parent or the spouse, grieving over the loss. After they bury their hero, they get the call: "pay up, the entire loan balance is due." No, you did nothing wrong. Yes, the borrower just died for their country. Yes, the whole reason the borrower got the loan in the first place is no longer valid, since the borrower is deceased and that degree is now useless. Nevermind all that. The borrower triggered the death and bankruptcy clause.

These clauses are not in *every* private student loan contract, but they are quite common, and they should give borrowers and cosigners pause. If you must have a cosigner, your best option is someone who is young and healthy with very stable finances, because if anything happens to him or her during your repayment term, you could be (to put it in lawyerly terms) screwed.

TIP: The so-called "death and bankruptcy" clause is not in federal student loan contracts. If a Parent PLUS borrower declares bankruptcy, for instance, it should not trigger default either for the parent borrower, or for the student for whom the loan was disbursed.

Cosigner Release

As I've said repeatedly, if the borrower cannot or does not pay the cosigned student loan, the cosigner is still on the hook. And the "death and bankruptcy clause" can be quite dangerous for either party. That clause is particularly worrisome where a borrower has a private loan cosigned by an elderly grandparent, or a parent is the cosigner on a private loan where the student can't pay because of a serious hardship.

Luckily, there may be a way out. Some private lenders allow for something called a *cosigner release*, where the lender lets the cosigner off the hook under certain conditions. These conditions vary from lender to lender, and the specifics may be outlined in the loan's original promissory note. In my experience, they come in two forms:

1. **Buyout**: a single lump-sum payment by the cosigner.
2. **Temporary installment arrangement**: a series of on-time monthly payments by the cosigner over the course of 12 to 48 months (depending on the lender and the loan terms).

If the conditions are met, the cosigner may be released from all legal responsibility on the loan, leaving the borrower as the sole signer. Remember that this not only protects the cosigner from being sued later, but also protects the borrower if the cosigner dies or declares bankruptcy.

If you are a cosigner or borrower and you are concerned about the long-term financial stability or health of the other signer on the loan, a cosigner release may be a good pre-emptive measure to protect yourself from an unnecessary (and, arguably, unfair) default. Review your loan promissory note and contact your private student loan lender or servicer to get some more information about the process and requirements.

Cosigner buyouts may be possible even for loans in default. These are almost always settlements requiring a lump-sum payment (rather than an installment plan). The amount that the cosigner pays in a post-default scenario may be significantly less than a cosigner buyout while the loan is in good standing, but this is not a suggestion to voluntarily default on the loan to get a "better deal." A pre-default cosigner release provides some safety for the borrower by making it impossible to trigger the "death and bankruptcy" clause, but it is mostly for the security of the cosigner. A post-default cosigner release won't undo the default, even if the default was triggered by the cosigner.

Keep in mind that after a cosigner release, the borrower is still on the hook for the remaining loan balance. And if the loan is in default, the borrower will still be subjected to collections actions. It's essentially a "save yourself" option.

TIP: Cosigner releases are often "discretionary." Even if they are permitted by your loan promissory note, the lender or loan holder is not obligated to grant one. So even if you do everything right, the request for the release could ultimately be denied.

Tips for Prospective and Current Cosigners

If you've read to this point, you'll probably agree with me on this: cosigning a private student loan may be a very bad idea. If you are thinking about cosigning, here are some tips:

- DON'T DO IT. Seriously. There are no benefits for you. It may be true that the borrower cannot get a lower interest rate without a cosigner. If the borrower's credit is bad or even just mediocre, he or she may not be able to take out the loan without a cosigner. It's heartbreaking. But cosigning a private student loan entails a lot of risk with no measurable payoff or benefit to the cosigner.
- If you're going to cosign anyway, only do so for someone who you know very well, someone you trust, someone you're going to maintain contact with for the entirety of the repayment period. Don't cosign for an acquaintance, a new friend, a distant cousin, a new boyfriend or girlfriend, or even worse, someone you don't really know at all. When you cosign a student loan, you are taking on thousands of dollars of debt with this person. Ask yourself: would you buy a home with the borrower? Would you open a business with the borrower? Would you personally lend this person a significant amount of money? Think carefully before you sign.
- Don't cosign unless you are in a financial position to make the monthly payments yourself on a long-term basis or pay the entire loan balance off in a lump sum. If there's a slight hiccup with the borrower's repayments, you will be subject to the same consequences as the borrower, including negative credit reporting, collections actions, and even a lawsuit. The borrower, as a recent grad or young professional, is unlikely

to be able to pay off the entire balance, so you may have to step in and make the monthly payments, or pay the loan off in full in order to avoid default. And we've already explored what *that* scenario looks like.

If you've already cosigned a student loan, here are some things to consider:

- Keep a good relationship with the borrower. Keep in contact, no matter what. I've seen relationships break down before any problems come up. When the borrower goes into default, the cosigner doesn't even know about it until the collections calls begin. In other scenarios, the relationship between the borrower and the cosigner sours when the borrower can't make his or her payments. Both scenarios are awful. The cosigner and the borrower are in this together. It's in your interest to be on the same page, to work together to obtain a resolution, and to be on the same side.
- In the same vein, I sometimes get calls from cosigners who want to take legal action against the borrower because the borrower defaulted on the loan, causing damage to the cosigner's credit report. First of all, if you have any relationship with the borrower, a lawsuit against them would almost certainly destroy it. Second, unless there is some sort of written agreement between you and the borrower, any such legal action may be tough to win (remember, you signed a loan contract that says you're both legally responsible for the loan). I don't take on these types of cases myself, but if you're looking for an attorney, contact your state bar association for a referral.
- Even if the borrower is making on-time payments, keep track of the loan. You wouldn't just ignore your credit card bill, or your monthly mortgage/rent obligation, would you? You don't just set aside your electric bill or insurance premium, right? Since you are equally legally responsible for this student loan, it's in your best interest to keep an eye on things. Don't just assume that the borrower will let you know about problems. Actively monitor the loan's repayment, and

at the first sign of trouble, get in touch with the borrower to figure out what's going on.

- If you're worried about the long-term viability of repaying the cosigned loan because one of you is becoming ill or financially unstable, start investigating your options for a cosigner release now. Don't wait until the loan is delinquent or in default. The borrower can also look into private student loan consolidation or refinancing. Consolidating or refinancing the underlying loan through a new private loan program could pay off that underlying loan, effectively releasing any cosigner from the obligation and creating a new loan where only the student borrower is legally responsible. You'll obviously want to confirm this outcome with your current loan holder and the prospective loan consolidation or refinancing company. If you can get yourself off the loan you've already signed, you will thank yourself later if anything goes wrong.

PART III: Conclusions

In 2014, the Obama administration proposed major changes to federal student loan repayment and forgiveness programs. These changes including expanding the Pay-As-You-Earn plan, arguably the most affordable income-driven repayment option, so that it is available to many more federal student loan borrowers.

But not Parent PLUS loan borrowers.

The administration is also calling for other changes to these income-driven plans, such as modifications to the payment calculation for married borrowers, increases in student loan payments for high-income earners, and caps on the Public Service Loan Forgiveness program. Around the same time, the House of Representatives proposed changes to the tax code that would eliminate some tax deductions for tuition and the repayment of student loans, while imposing additional taxes on certain federal student loan repayment programs.

None of those proposed reforms affect cosigners or Parent PLUS borrowers.

Other bills filed in Congress during the last few years have proposed expanding federal student loan forgiveness and consolidation programs, eliminating those same programs, allowing borrowers to refinance their student loans at lower interest rates, raising the interest rates on federal student loans, and deducting student loan payments directly from borrowers' paychecks.

Most of those proposed reforms, even the good ones, do not even mention cosigners or Parent PLUS borrowers.

So what's the takeaway?

First of all, I have an opinion about Parent PLUS loans and cosigned private loans, if you can't tell by now: federal Parent PLUS loans and cosigned private student loans just stink. These are terrible loans, and while people take them out with the best of intentions, it often comes back to bite them (and then they wind up in my office).

And while there is growing recognition that student loan debt is becoming a crushing burden, the focus right now is largely on the students. That's not necessarily wrong; millions of students *are* being crushed by unsustainable levels of student debt, which is hindering their ability to fully participate in society. But parents and cosigners are not a major part of the national conversation right now.

Thankfully, that is beginning to change. Part of that change is coming from you. You are telling your stories. You are sharing your experiences. As more of you do this, people are noticing.

News reports about private student loan lenders aggressively pursuing the cosigners of deceased military service members led to a huge public outcry. Some lenders started to change their policies and conduct as a result. Family members were saved from the horror of burying loved ones while fielding harassing phone calls from student loan collections agencies.

Similarly, in late 2014, news reports showed that private student loan lenders were refusing to work with troubled borrowers and cosigners. As a direct result, several major private student loan lenders began offering loan modifications, similar to home mortgage modifications. While these programs are new and very small-scale, they have allowed some troubled borrowers and cosigners to stay afloat and avoid default. This is a huge shift, and I'm really hoping it's a sign of things to come.

Despite all the bad stuff about Parent PLUS loans and cosigner rights, I am optimistic about the future. The current system, and the current way of doing things, is just not sustainable. I think we will see some positive reforms to student loans in the coming years. While it may take longer than we'd hope, some of these reforms will inevitably benefit parent borrowers and cosigners, as well as students.

So stay strong. Arm yourself with information. Avoid these situations if you can, and if it's too late for that, take advantage of the programs that are out there now, even if they're imperfect. Share your stories. And remember: you are more than your debt. Don't let it control your life.

Resources

The federal student loan database (the "National Student Loan Data System"):
www.nslds.ed.gov.

The federal government's web portal for loan consolidation and repayment plan selection:
www.studentloans.gov

The National Consumer Law Center has lots of free information for student loan borrowers:
www.nclc.org

The National Association of Consumer Advocates is an organization of consumer rights attorneys. They have a directory on their website if you're looking for an attorney:
www.naca.net

Follow my blog!
www.BostonStudentLoanLawyer.com

About the Author

Adam S. Minsky founded the first law office in Massachusetts devoted entirely to assisting student loan borrowers, and he is one of the only attorneys in the country practicing in this area of law. Atty. Minsky provides counsel, legal assistance, and direct advocacy for borrowers on a variety of student loan-related matters, including student loan management, administrative disputes with loan holders, and default prevention and resolution. He has been interviewed by major national publications including *The New York Times*, *The Wall Street Journal*, *Bloomberg News*, *Kiplinger's Personal Finance Magazine*, and *The Chronicle of Higher Education*, and he has published multiple articles on student loan-related topics. Atty. Minsky has also served as faculty for continuing legal education seminars on the topic of student loan law, and he regularly speaks to students, graduates, and advocates about the latest developments in higher education financing. He maintains a nationally recognized blog on student loan-related issues at www.BostonStudentLoanLawyer.com.

Atty. Minsky received his undergraduate degree, with honors, from Boston University, and his law degree from Northeastern University School of Law. He is a member of the National Association of Consumer Advocates. Atty. Minsky lives near Boston, Massachusetts.

Made in the USA
Las Vegas, NV
15 February 2021

17892258R00031